MAN OR MALE?

Philip Ganzfried

First Edition

ISBN: 978-1-686-59677-3

Table of Contents

Foreword

The Lord was developing this book in Philip's heart for fifteen years, and in early 2019, impressed on him the need to complete it. I am adding this foreword to share with you the devastating news that Philip died suddenly and unexpectedly in his sleep on Thursday, September 5, 2019, twelve days after he completed this book.

He was thirty-two years old.

Philip was my son, my brother in Christ, and my dear friend. We shared everything. Challenges. Victories. Philip had wisdom beyond his years. He loved his mom and his three sisters. And as the oldest child, he was such a good example to them. His heart called for men to be strong leaders, husbands, and fathers, and he led by example.

God brought Philip and his wife, Jennifer, together through improbable circumstances. Their love was immediate and grew stronger every day. They were truly a match made in Heaven. Philip was a very proud father who loved his children with all his heart. He was a great daddy! Please pray for this young family.

Our families take great comfort in knowing that Philip is in the presence of our Lord and Savior Jesus Christ, but there is a huge, irreparable hole in our hearts. Our faith and the innumerable prayers of our family and friends are so greatly appreciated and are what sustains us through this difficult time.

This book was written for men by a true man, a

man after God's own heart. Philip's legacy will go on through his family, those who knew him, those who heard about him, and hopefully those who are encouraged by this book.

Tom Ganzfried

Chapter Zero:
Introduction & Warnings

When someone loses their grip on reality and begins acting crazy, sometimes a slap in the face can be appropriate and necessary to bring them back into focus. Our culture has lost its grip on reality. This book may be the slap in the face that we need. It's a defibrillator shock to get our mindset back into rhythm with the truth.

This book is addressed to all guys of all ages and all walks of life. Young guys, old guys, single dudes, married dudes, kids and gents with kids. This is for all of us and we're all in it together!

If you're easily offended, buckle up; I'm going to offend you so get over it now. Exactly why **you need this book**. This is going to push you out of your comfort zone; because if someone doesn't get their nice, little, cozy bubble popped, then they'll never step out of it to change and grow.

If you're already wondering why you let someone talk you into reading this book, then do me a favor before you put it down: think of someone that you care about; maybe someone who depends on you or you look up to— it may be a child, a wife/girlfriend, a parent, a sibling or a friend. Find a picture of them right now and stare into their eyes in the picture. Do it for them. Do it to be a better man for your loved ones. Do it for yourself. Just do it.

You will notice that I seek outside wisdom a lot. The ancient King of Israel, Solomon, is recorded in multiple historical accounts to be the wisest man to ever live. Fortunately for us, he left a book of his wise sayings behind, so I will quote from his book often. Wise guidance will be the key to gleaning the most out of this book.

This has been on my heart for over 15 years, so stick with me and let's dig into one of the biggest problems that's affecting our culture and world today: the sheer lack of true manhood. This might be a wild ride for some of you, but I believe that this is exactly what you need to hear right now. This book is short because manhood isn't complicated when it's broken down into simple parts and analyzed. Let's dig in together and discover what it takes to **BE A REAL MAN**!

-Philip Ganzfried

PS: To any lady reading this: yes, there are practical principles in here that can be extracted for your benefit as well, but it is directed towards guys. If you are single, I hope that this book gives you a better idea of what you should be looking for in a husband before you settle for just a male. If you are married, then I hope this book helps your husband become the real man that you both need him to be—you should read it together! This book is short, but it's not sweet. Please feel free to ignore the manly musk and enjoy the journey with us!

Chapter One: Misconception of Manhood

The biggest misconception about manhood is that just being born a *male* is enough to make you a *man*. Guys, there is a Grand Canyon of a difference between being a **male** and being a **man**. **All men are males, but not all males are real men**.

Being a male is easy. It's simple science. Each cell in the human body contains 23 pairs of chromosomes; 22 of those are the same between males and females but the last pair determines your gender—either XY or XX. The presence of the Y chromosome creates male parts;

therefore, you are either born with or without a Y sex chromosome. Being a male is easy but too many people stop there and expect manhood to come just as easily and naturally.

Manhood is not tied to age. The misconception that you magically become a man at a certain point stops guys from pursuing it further. After all, why would you work hard for something that you would get automatically without any effort? If only that was the case, but it's not. **Manhood doesn't happen by accident. True manhood takes *intentional determination* and *ongoing hard work*.**

Let's take a quick look at a few comparative examples of guys of all ages:

A 19-year-old who shows respect by holding the door for an elderly woman is showing his manhood.

A 40-year-old who shows foolishness by disregarding wise counsel shows his lack of manhood.

A 60-year-old who shows humility by admitting mistakes and improving himself shows his manhood.

A 25-year-old who shows arrogance by thinking he knows it all shows his lack of manhood.

A 17-year-old who shows wisdom by obeying sound advice shows his manhood.

A 36-year-old who shows disrespect by hitting a woman shows his lack of manhood.

Clearly manhood is not about age; so, what is manhood? Why can a young man have it before an old fool does? Who can know where to look to acquire it? How will you know when you're really a man and not just a male? These are all valid questions and observations but don't feel overwhelmed because we will tackle it all one piece at a time as we break down manhood into simple parts.

Our culture's view of manhood is so broken that if you search Google for "aspects of manhood," six of the top 10 results (at the time of my search) didn't even include the word "manhood" but instead were just about "masculinity" (with the top result being Wikipedia's page titled "masculinity"). We're so blinded by maleness that we don't see the glaring difference between the two. Womanhood doesn't carry quite as much of a connotative difference between it and being a female; but **manhood** should have a strong weightiness to it that distinguishes the difference between being a **man** and just being a *male*.

For starters, let's look at what manhood is not. Masculinity is what most guys think of right away—it's the love of things like hunting, fishing and being outdoors; it's the drive to be the best at sports or competitions; it's the passion for building, creating or concurring things; it's the desire to get rough, tough and dirty all over. Masculinity is important, for sure; but it shouldn't be the only focus. Maleness and masculinity have run rampant as the primary source of manhood for far too long. We need to balance both masculinity and true manhood.

Let's take a look behind the curtain of true manhood and see what makes it so rare these days. **It's interestingly *inclusive* because it is available for ALL guys of ALL ages from ALL walks of life and yet it's entirely *exclusive* because only those who <u>choose to seek it</u> will ever find it and become a real man**. In the next few chapters we're going to explore some different aspects of manhood and what it takes to acquire it intentionally. We're going to build a foundation for you to grow and develop your manhood!

[Side note: The previous list of things like sports and outdoor stuff is not exclusive to just guys; females can have all of the same likes and desires and still maintain their femaleness. A fully masculine male and a fully feminine female can enjoy the same activities. Men and women share similar character traits and values.]

Chapter Two: Humility of a Hammer

You're a tool. You probably don't hear that enough from other people, so I'll say it again: you are a tool. We're all tools. We are all designed to be used in a specific way for a specific reason.

As the book cover so accurately explains, a hammer is not a drill. A nail is not a screw. That's pretty simple for most people to understand, but we don't realize how much it applies to our lives as well. When something is being built, every part of the job requires a different type of tool. You don't paint with a crowbar or measure with a hard hat. In the same way, humans are all created with a specific set of gifts and abilities; and we're created for a specific role or task. When this is forgotten, it leads to two different issues: **jealousy** and **arrogance**.

A hammer doesn't get jealous because it can't cut as well as a saw—it knows its purpose. When we compare ourselves to others and wish we had what they have or were what they are, we open ourselves up to jealousy and insecurity. What you need to understand is that every tool is important and vital to the job. From the janitor to the CEO, every role in an organization is needed. There is a crucial part for every person to play. We shouldn't compare ourselves to others in a way that makes us jealous or envious. If everyone at a company was a CEO, then there wouldn't be a sales staff to bring in profits or a janitorial staff to keep the office clean; and the company would stink—figuratively and physically!

The other side of that coin is when we arrogantly compare ourselves to others and think we are more important. Does it really matter if the drill or the ladder is used more often? Does it matter which tool is used at the very beginning and which is used at the very end? Of course not! It sounds ridiculous to compare tools like that because nothing would be finished without ALL the tools working together. So why would one tool think they're better than the others?

When someone looks at a new building, do they praise the hammer that was used? Not at all. The *builder* gets the credit—not the tools that were used. So again, let me say: you're a tool. **You need to understand that you were created for a specific reason, with specific talents and with a vital role to fill**. Once you understand that, you can see the folly of comparing yourself to others in a jealous or arrogant way. The correct response to both is humility.

Humility combats both jealousy and arrogance and helps build a foundation of manhood. Humility gives us strength because it prevents the insecurity of jealousy and the blindness of arrogance. The root word for humility is "to know your place." When we embrace humility and truly know our place, we gain a clearer understanding of the people and world around us.

When we compare ourselves to others and decide that we are less than them, it lowers our self-esteem and causes pain and strife—sometimes internally and sometimes externally. But there is no reason to put yourself down or think less of yourself when you understand true humility and the power that it provides. **Humility is not thinking less of yourself; humility is thinking of yourself less.**[1]

Again, we all have a purpose in life. Knowing your role and where you fit in can be liberating and encouraging. It all starts with humility.

I was once in a tactical training course and the instructor told me to "keep my head on a swivel." What he meant by that was don't just stare straight ahead at your target, but instead always be turning your head and looking around. You need to know what is ahead of you just as much as what is behind, beside and above you. It is called 'situational awareness' and it is crucial for manhood. *Arrogance creates blindness*; but the dangerous part is that it does it in such a way that we don't think we're blind when we really are. **Humility is the 'head on a swivel' that helps us open our eyes to see what is truly going on around us**. A man who fully understands what's around him will know how to respond to situations that others cannot. There is strength in that.

Another aspect of humility is that it is like the fertilizer that helps us grow. Ernest Hemingway said, "There is nothing noble in being superior to your fellow man; true nobility is being superior to your former self."[2] If you want to grow or improve at anything in life—sports, skills, job, manhood, etc.—you must be humble enough to know and admit that you have room for growth and improvement. If you already think of yourself in first place, there's nowhere to go. If you are humble enough to recognize your place and keep pushing yourself to grow, you will. You have to look at where you are now and be humble enough to know it's not where you want to be so that you can improve. Then you can look back and 'feel superior to your former self' as Hemingway put it—as long as you don't forget to stay humble and keep growing still.

There are many other aspects of humility as well that you should dig into and study later. There is a great book called Humility: True Greatness by C. J. Mahaney *(I have no affiliation with it or him)* that can help you dig deeper into the strength that comes from humility.

So be humble. Compare your current self to your future self, but don't compare yourself to others: whether you think you are better than them or less than them. **We are all created equal but different** and we were all created with specific gifts and abilities. Know your role and wield the power of humility to see the world like a real man. The humility of a hammer will give you the first piece of the foundation of manhood.

Chapter Three:
Wise Guy

The next piece of the foundation of manhood is wisdom. A male and a man approach wisdom differently. Like manhood, people erroneously assume wisdom comes automatically with age—but it's not that easy. Usually around a birthday, people may say they're "older and wiser" now that another year has gone by; but in reality, wisdom is also something that has to be intentionally sought after and worked on. While, yes, it does take time to acquire, that doesn't mean it comes naturally or automatically. You must choose to pursue it daily. The stereotypical "old fool" proves that you don't magically get wisdom with old age. Mark Twain said, "I was young and foolish then; now I am old and foolisher."[3]

Let's step back and explain what wisdom really is. Wisdom is not intelligence or smarts. It is not just information or knowledge. Essentially, **wisdom is the ability to apply knowledge to a situation**. *You can have knowledge without wisdom, but you cannot have wisdom without knowledge.* Some people are born naturally wiser than others, but everyone has the capacity to seek and gain wisdom throughout life.

Socrates said, "The only true wisdom is in knowing you know nothing."[4] It's a little extreme, but it basically means the more you know about something, the more you realize there is so much more that you don't know. It is actually meant as an encouragement to keep learning more. You can never have enough knowledge or wisdom.

The way a man seeks wisdom intentionally is by starting with the humility we just talked about. The ancient King Solomon, known for being the wisest person to ever live, once said, "Pride leads to disgrace, but with humility comes wisdom."[5] We've already seen the importance of humility and how it counters jealousy and arrogance, but at the same time it also goes hand in hand with gaining wisdom.

Humility allows us to step back from a situation and analyze what is going on (head on a swivel style). Understanding the situation and environment around you is what leads to applying knowledge properly and wisely. That is practical wisdom in action.

Practical wisdom is something anybody can pursue over a lifetime as long as they have the right humility and mindset. But where it really matters is what we'll call *true wisdom.* True wisdom is not based on knowledge obtained by life experiences like practical wisdom, but instead is uniquely given by God to anyone who asks Him for it. **It is simultaneously the easiest and hardest type of wisdom to get. All you have to do is ask for it, but at the same time you have to be humble enough to ask for it honestly.** Quoting from King Solomon again:

"Only God gives wisdom; from His mouth come knowledge and understanding."

"It is better to get wisdom than gold, and understanding is better than silver!"

"The one who gets wisdom loves life; the one who cherishes understanding will soon prosper."

"The way of a fool is right in his own eyes, but a wise man listens to advice."[6]

According to historical records, King Solomon reigned from 970 to 931 BC. During that time, he amassed a treasury unlike anyone else in history. It is said that in addition to countless livestock, silver and gems, he had at least 40,000 lbs. of gold. Popular economists estimate his personal wealth in present-day value at a staggering $2.1 TRILLION.[7] He was ***unparalleled*** in his wealth and influence, and yet, even he knew that wisdom was more valuable and important than gold. Other kings and dignitaries would come to him for advice and counsel and they would bring gifts from all over the world. That is one of the ways he became so financially prosperous. But through all of the glamor and fame, he still knew that the source of his wealth and wisdom was from God.

Do you know any foolish people that are actually happy with their lives? Most may pretend to be but deep down they long for something else. Some people may even be wealthy—either from an inheritance or earned through hard work and knowledge—but without wisdom's guidance, they are more likely to lose it, waste it or just live life without the fullness of joy. **Wisdom is the key to unlocking the greatness of life**. Seek wisdom above everything else.

If practical wisdom is like a skill that you learn over time, then true wisdom is like the muscle memory that makes using that skill easier and more effective. They go hand in hand to strengthen the wielder. Practical wisdom takes humility and a lifetime of intentional pursuit; true wisdom takes humility and a willingness to seek God. Both are vital parts of manhood and both are crucial to having a truly great life. Seeking both aspects of wisdom will give you the second piece of the foundation of manhood.

Chapter Four:
Uncommon Common Sense

Common sense is such an oxymoron. Good sense is so uncommon that it's borderline rare these days. As I mentioned in the Humility chapter, the phrase 'keep your head on a swivel' is often used in the military to enforce that you need to always look around you in all directions. You must take in your entire surrounding in order to process the best way to approach what is in front of you. That applies to every aspect of our daily lives.

Common sense is what gives you the ability to see your surroundings and not just what is right in front of you. It's called 'situational awareness' and it is crucial to manhood. If you're so fixated on what you're looking at that you can't see what's coming from outside your field of view, you're going to get blindsided. We teach kids from a very early age that if you cross a busy street without looking both ways, you'll get run over by a car. If you're a football player who only looks at the guy in front of you, you'll get run over by a car-size linebacker from the side. If you're a manager at work who makes decisions that affect other people without calculating the impact to every area of the company, it's not going to go well for you. Every part of life requires us to analyze our situation and make good judgement calls based on the information around us. In business, it's called being a Global Thinker and it means looking at all of the data from different perspectives and understanding how something will impact the situation for everyone.

Common sense is also called ***understanding*** or ***discernment***. Throughout his whole book of wise sayings, King Solomon often puts Wisdom and Understanding together and compares the pair against what he calls a fool. He said this about them both:

“[Make] your ear attentive to wisdom and inclining your heart to understanding.”

“Fools despise wisdom and instruction.”

“A fool takes no pleasure in understanding.”

“[God] gives wisdom; from His mouth come knowledge and understanding.”

“Blessed is the one who finds wisdom, and the one who gets understanding.”

“On the lips of him who has understanding, wisdom is found, but a rod is for the back of him who lacks sense.”

“Do not be like the horse or the mule, which have no understanding but must be controlled by bit and bridle or they will not come to you.”[8]

Again, King Solomon regularly puts wisdom and understanding together in his book. As I just said in the Wisdom chapter, “wisdom is the ability to apply knowledge to a situation;” but to put it another way: **Wisdom is knowing <u>WHAT</u> to do. Understanding/discernment is knowing the <u>who, where, when and how</u> of what to do**. That is why they go hand in hand.

When you're able to understand what is around you and properly apply wisdom to the situation, that is discernment. But if discernment is what allows us to have common sense and make good decisions, why do so many people try to go through life without it? Why are so many people content with repeatedly making poor judgment choices?

Without the foundation of manhood, males are content to make willy-nilly decisions without thinking through the outcomes it brings. Will it affect more than just you? Will it harm others? **Will there be short-term gains but long-term pains?** You need to keep your head on a swivel, know your surroundings and make smart decisions about what you do or say.

Another ancient quote says, "Who is wise and understanding among you? Let them show it by their good life, by deeds done in the humility that comes from wisdom."[9] When wisdom and discernment are a core part of your life, it will be obvious by how you live. You can usually look at a person and know pretty quickly if they're making good choices with their life or poor judgment choices and are suffering the consequences. That doesn't mean you can always judge a book by its cover, but it does mean that improve your life by basing your decisions on sound wisdom and discernment.

When you take the time to step back from a situation and humbly try to understand what is going on around you, then you are able to know what to do, when to do it, where to do it, why to do it, how to do it and who to do it with. Seeking that discernment will give you the third piece of the foundation of manhood.

Chapter Five:
Grow Up

With humility, wisdom and discernment in place, the next piece of the foundation of manhood is maturity. Our culture has grown increasingly immature over the last few decades and it continues to decline. If we don't start maturing quickly, the damage will continue cascading downward.

Historically, there were only two age categories: young boys and grown men. There was a defining moment that separated those two—a rite of passage or declaration. Sadly, that clear line in the sand has been lost and we are left with a recently created third category called adolescence. Adolescence is a phase between child and adult that is so undefined that some people make it "through" in a few years and others take a few decades. That's why we have guys in their 20s and 30s that still act like children. Some never grow out of their childish ways.

Like wisdom, maturity is not automatically tied to getting older. Maturity is actually relative to age and is simply *acting your age*. **It is okay to act like a five-year-old when you are five; it is not okay to act like a five-year-old when you are 25**. You can be a mature 12-year-old at the age of 12. You can't be a mature 12-year-old at the age of 30! But if you're 30 acting like 30, then it's a good thing! And of course, being more mature than your age is great.

The difference between a mature man and an immature boy is that a mature man takes responsibility for his actions. Taking responsibility for yourself, and often those around you, shows who you really are inside. That means if you make a mistake, whether you are nine or 99, you admit the mistake and own up to it. Blaming others or passing the buck are ways that immature boys try to avoid consequences. **All actions have consequences and mature men take responsibility for their actions**.

We physically grow up automatically, but we need to grow our maturity intentionally. We see kids getting stuck in this limbo phase of adolescence without clear guidance on how to complete it and mature. Throughout history and in cultures all around the world today, there have been countless different rites of passage, sometimes called a Coming of Age ritual, where a boy becomes a man. There was a clear point in their life that signified they were no longer a child and had grown up. With that came a new level of expectations and responsibility that forced them to mature quickly. In a small tribe that relies on hunting for food, this may mean a 13-year-old boy is now joining the tribal hunt and is expected to carry their weight—literally—or put the whole tribe at risk of starvation or attack. That will definitely help mature a boy quickly!

In today's society, we lack that defining moment that forces boys to mature and grow up and the result is we have immature 23-year-old boys that live at home and selfishly mooch off of their parents. Or we have immature 33-year-old boys that are sleeping around and impregnating women that they aren't married to and are not taking responsibility for their actions. **Our culture has shown that anyone can be immature at any age. But the good news is that anyone can also be *mature* at any age as well!** Without that defining line in the sand, we are forced to mature on our own (or if you're blessed to have a mature father, he can guide you).

Since you can be mature at any age and immature at any age; let's see what acting your age actually looks like practically:

As a teenager, it means obeying your parents and listening to their advice. As much as you hate to admit it, your parents have been around a lot longer than you and know a lot of things that you don't. A mature teenager recognizes that and listens to their advice even when it doesn't seem cool. And if you're responsible for chores, then do them without having to be asked three times—or better yet, do them without having to be asked at all! If you're not responsible for chores, that doesn't mean you can't step up and help out. Show your parents your young manhood by offering to help them with something. If you see your mom struggling to keep the house clean, then shock her by randomly vacuuming the house one day. She will be so blessed to see her little man stepping up and helping on his own initiative! She will respect you so much more for it!

Another way to show your maturity is in honesty. If you make a mistake or do something wrong (lie, cheat, steal, etc.), the best thing you can do is confess it openly to your parents (or boss) before you are found out later. "Truth builds trust. Disclosure is better than Discovery."[10] When they find out on their own, you lose their trust—when are upfront and honest with a humble heart of repentance, you gain their trust even when you mess up. Trust is always built slowly and lost quickly, but maturity is a great way to boost trust with people.

As a young adult without kids, it means being responsible and pursing a future full-time career. You may or may not have done (or are doing) college or a trade-school, but it means you're not just nonchalantly jumping from job to job because you're lazy and not willing to work (or be in school). This is the time in your life when you'll have the time to focus on growing and improving yourself, so take advantage of it!

As an adult with young kids, it means being a provider and protector of your family. By this point in life, you should have (or be pursing) a full-time job and career. You should have a vision for your life and know where you want to end up in a few decades. Usually your vision will change as you age, but at least you're on a path forward and not just flippantly flipping burgers and trying to coast through life. [If you and your wife have decided that it is better that she will work and you will stay home with the kids, that is admirable and does not make you less of a man.] But in most cases, you will be the primary source of income for your family and providing for them will be *your* job. This means you care for your family more than yourself. **If you're driving a $30,000 car and your family can't afford food or normal necessities—you have a major problem with your priorities**. Having a working vacuum or stove at home is more important than having a new set of shiny rims for your ride. Your family always comes first. YOU are their provider and protector. **You care for your family's needs—physically, mentally, emotionally and spiritually —even if it costs you some personal comfort or pain**. They are your priority. Financial guru Dave Ramsey, says, "It's a sign of maturity when you delay pleasure today so that you can ensure a better tomorrow."[11] Provide for your family now and in the future. Don't just think about yourself or just think about today. Your family needs you to be the man in charge and lead them in the right direction for the rest of their lives.

As a protector of your family, this also means having life insurance and a legal will in place—neither one takes very long to set up and they can save your family a LOT of stress and pain if you die unexpectedly. Do it asap and give everyone some peace of mind.

Additionally, these are the most important years in your children's lives, and they need you in their lives now as much as ever. Be present when you're with them—this is hard for me as well because in this day and age we are all addicted to our smartphones; but it means putting it down when you're with your kids and focusing on time with them. Your kids don't care how much money you make or what car you drive; they just care about being with you and spending time with their loving daddy. You make all the difference to them just by being present and kind. So, stop worry and stressing about life and just live life to its fullest with those who love you no matter what you do!

As an adult with teens or older kids, this is the time to start helping them build their own foundation of manhood (or womanhood) and crossing over that line into full adulthood so they're not stuck in adolescence forever. **They need YOU to lead them over the line by example**. They will do what they see you doing, so make sure it's the right thing.

As an adult with older kids (or without kids at all), your focus should be on growing your relationship with your wife. If you're a new empty-nester, don't let the fact that the kids are now gone cause you and your wife to fall apart or grow distant. This is the time to rekindle any lost romance and pursue your wife like you did when you first met. You will be so glad that you now have time to "date" your wife again, so take advantage of it and enjoy life together as best friends!

As a veteran adult, you should be fully prepared for the future financially and legally. Make sure your kids are on the right path in life and make sure that you are leaving behind a legacy that will last for generations and not be forgotten. Be a source of love and joy for those around you and not a source of stress or pain. Oscar Wilde said, "Some cause happiness wherever they go; others *whenever* they go."[12] Make your legacy matter when you're gone! We all make mistakes in life, but don't let pride or arrogance stop you from undoing those mistakes where you can.

We have to intentionally strive for maturity every day as we grow up. Our actions are our own, our thoughts are our own, our words are our own. Everything we do, think or say are our doing and we must take responsibility for them. Someone who shoplifts at 15 and doesn't take responsibility for their actions, could end up embezzling from their company at 55. Taking responsibility is about learning from your mistakes and growing up. When you do that, you mature and act appropriately for your age.

Nobody wants to be around a 40-year-old guy who throws tantrums like a five-year-old baby. Nobody wants to hire a 30-year-old guy who has the lazy, entitled mindset of a 12-year-old boy. Maturity is so important to living well. When you grow up and take responsibility for yourself, that maturity will give you the fourth piece of the foundation of manhood.

Chapter Six:
Tough 'n Tender

With humility, wisdom, discernment and maturity in place, the last piece of the foundation of manhood is emotional strength. This has nothing to do with physical strength or size. It doesn't matter if you are tall or short, thick or thin, beefy or a pipsqueak; no matter your physical conditions, you can always be a real man and flex your emotional muscles.

Far too often males measure and compare themselves by their grunts, chest bumps and high-fives. They think becoming a man means gaining the ability to smash a beer can on their head and grow some hair on their chin. Really?! Why would anyone think that is all there is to being a man? It's not just about catching the largest fish or kicking the farthest ball. Physical accomplishments are a great thing to have or strive towards, but there is so much more to it than that. To really be a man, you must also be *emotionally* strong. **Emotional strength is expressed in multiple ways—we'll look at a few of them: self-control, love, apologeticness and sorrow**.

The first way emotional strength is expressed is in self-control. Self-control is such a broad term and can apply to nearly every part of life, but it is specifically vital when dealing with emotions. Is it okay to get angry? Absolutely. Is it okay to explode with anger and lash out physically or verbally? Absolutely not. Losing your temper is one of the most common ways of demonstrating a *lack* of self-control. Anger is a natural emotion that we all have but it doesn't have to control us. We need to control *it*. **A real man doesn't have to resort to violence or yelling to solve problems**. As a caveat, I will add that, yes, there is an *occasional* time and place where getting angry and lashing out physically is acceptable—if you're walking down the street and you see someone getting mugged in an alley, I give you permission to get angry and rush in to help. Other than that, it's very rarely an acceptable thing to lash out—and most importantly, it should never be directed at your family. You can get frustrated at something or someone without letting it turn into full anger—as long as you are self-controlled. "Fools vent their anger, but the wise quietly hold it back."[13] **Self-control flexes your emotional muscles proudly**!

Another aspect of self-control is in protecting yourself from adultery. This should go without saying, but I'll say it anyway: it is not okay to cheat on your wife with someone else. Ever. I won't beat a dead horse with something that should be so obvious. **If you're having sex with someone that is not your wife, I'll be blunt: you've lost your manhood**. Go back to the start of the book and try again. Do not pass Go. Do not collect $200. Adultery is not okay and should not be tolerated. The solution is to protect yourself from lust with emotional self-control.

A second way emotional strength is expressed is in love. Love is a scary word for a lot of guys. Some people grew up without ever knowing love or what it was like to have a loving parent—especially a loving father. It may have even been a taboo topic that was never discussed.

But I'm here to tell you that **love MUST be a part of your life to truly grasp manhood**. Picture the most rough and tough biker gang member whose face has never shown any emotion other than anger; he may be covered in head to toe tattoos, but one of those is probably an "I love my mom" tat. *Everyone* has a natural love for their mom. So, if you can love your mother, why can't you love anyone else? Take that love for mom from down deep in your heart and let's make it stronger!

I was incredibly blessed to have been raised in a wonderful family with parents that love me. Nowadays that is a very rare thing and I don't take it for granted. Thanks to my upbringing, it is very natural for me to express love. I tell my wife and kids that I love them and then hug and kiss them at least a dozen times per day. I know that may not be something you are comfortable with, but it shows emotional strength. We shouldn't be afraid of our feelings or afraid to express our feelings—especially to our *loved* ones. They are called ***loved*** ones for a reason. *We love them.* So show it! **Stop what you are doing and go tell your wife or girlfriend that you love her and then kiss her. I don't mean a little peck on the cheek; I mean really kiss her. Hold it for five or six seconds and then tell her you love her again. Don't get too frisky though—this**

isn't about sex; it's about letting her know how much you love her. After that, go find your kids and kiss them on the forehead. I don't care if they're in pre-school, high school or grad school—they always need a kiss from Dad. They may resist, but that's where you get to flex your emotional muscles! Be the big *man!* Tell them you love them. Maybe you already have and it's normal or maybe they've never heard it from you and it will blow their minds. Either way, you are now on a new path that will open your eyes to a whole new world of love and excitement! You're welcome. (If they don't live near you, you can call them and tell them over the phone, but in-person is ideal if possible.) Theodore Hesburgh said, "The most important thing a father can do for his children is to love their mother."[14] So true! Your kids need to see you loving their mother for them to truly understand what love is for themselves.

Another aspect of expressing strength through love is in giving compliments. So many guys never or rarely compliment their wife/girlfriend or their kids. You would be amazed at how far a single complement each day can take your relationship. Go ahead and show off your manly emotional muscles again and give a genuine, whole-hearted compliment to your loved ones. Don't make it sexual—it's not about you, it's about them. A real compliment has to be about something she cares about: if she spent time getting ready in the morning, compliment her hair; if she spent time cleaning the house, compliment the great job she did; if she spent time making food, compliment the taste. Compliment how smart, caring, funny or organized she is; whatever you can think of that will tell her you care about her and are interested in HER. It may seem little and unimportant to you, but it will mean the world to her—as long as you are genuine and honest. You can complement her physical beauty as well but focus on her inner character first. Go on, give it a shot now—the book can wait!

A third way emotional strength is expressed is in the ability to apologize and ask for forgiveness. Our culture has turned the word "sorry" into an expression of weakness, but that couldn't be further from the truth. Being able to admit when you are wrong or made a mistake is a sign of emotional strength and maturity [see previous chapter]. If it's easier for you, use the phrase "I apologize" instead; but you must really mean it. Just loosely throwing around sorry or I apologize doesn't do any good if you don't express true remorse. Especially if you've hurt someone in the past, being apologetic can go a long way towards strengthening your emotional biceps.

It can start healing a relationship that has been damaged in the past or may prevent a relationship from being damaged in the future. And try this: apologize to your child and ask for their forgiveness. Ouch. What seems like a move that takes you a step back, is actually something that adds security in them and elevates the respect they have for you. If you think there's nothing you need to apologize for, wait about 30 minutes—you'll do something. If your child is young, kneel down to get to their eye-level and show them respect as you apologize. You will both grow from it in a way that you never dreamed possible.

A fourth way emotional strength is expressed is in how we handle sadness and sorrow. When a human gets sad, the lacrimal apparatus system next to the eyeball produces and drains tears. It's a perfectly normal and common part of our bodily functions and biology. So why do some people think that crying is a sign of weakness? Everybody gets sad. Everybody cries. It's a part of the human body and a natural part of life. We need to embrace it and not be afraid to show it. Let's look at an example of how to handle sadness and sorrow: we've talked about King Solomon, but his father, King David, was also a well-known historical figure.

King David was the ultimate Dude of Dudes. This guy was rough, tough and unstoppable. Let's look at his resumé:

- As the youngest of at least eight brothers, he was responsible for protecting the family livestock and flocks. As a teenager, it is reported that he killed multiple **bears** and **lions** with just a club while protecting the flocks.[15]
- Still as a teenager, he volunteered to help the army win a war by single-handedly defeating Goliath. Picture André the Giant, a French professional wrestler, who was over seven feet tall and built like a small house. Goliath was multiple feet taller than everyone else and yet young David took him down in one-on-one combat.[16]
- When David was older, he became the king and united the northern and southern tribes of Israel. He built a foundation that the nation of Israel has maintained for nearly 3,000 years.[17]
- He built an army of the strongest men and together won countless wars. Over the course of his life, it is said that he *personally* killed tens and tens of thousands of enemies.[18]

Clearly, this guy is one tough dude and knows how to throw down with the best of them. Let's look at what else he did:

- He cried. In his personal journal, he wrote: "I am worn out from sobbing. All night I flood my bed with weeping, drenching it with my tears."[19]
- He played multiple musical instruments like the lyre and nevel (both stringed instruments of that era).
- He wrote songs and poems. We have 73 of his songs/hymns recorded.[20] 73 is not a small number! And that's just what survived the last 3,000 years!

****Side note: there are more original historical manuscripts of King David and King Solomon from almost 3,000 years ago than there are from all 37 of Shakespeare's plays from 400 years ago combined!*[21]***

King David is an amazing example of what true manhood looks like. He's physically strong for sure, but more importantly, he's extremely emotionally strong. He gives a whole new meaning to "it takes a real man to show emotions." He's a mixed martial arts fighter who's never lost and yet he writes songs and poems about love, sorrow, frustration, anguish, joy and many other emotional moments of his life. **Guys, if the mighty King David can cry, then *we* can cry!**

I'm going to go one step further and say it's even okay to cry in front of our wives. Again, the false nomenclature is that crying shows weakness, but let me tell you what—**crying in front of your wife will show her a new side of you that will blow her mind**. She will love and respect you even more for it and you will be one step closer to realizing true manhood.

These fall into two categories of emotional strength: controlling your emotions and expressing your emotions. Everyone has emotions and feels the same emotions, but everyone reacts to them differently. Some guys yell and cause emotional harm to others, some guys hit and abuse and cause physical harm to others and other guys shove emotions down inside and try to ignore them but just end up causing harm to themselves. You have to deal with emotions properly and in a controlled way. Don't take it out on others incorrectly and don't take it out on yourself incorrectly. Self-control is how you control your emotions and then deal with them properly to help them grow into amazing emotions that you can then express to others. **Everyone wants to be loved by someone else, so BE the person that loves others and help them grow from it as well**!

Think of emotions like tools; you can't have just one! As psychologist Abraham Maslow said, "if the only tool you have is a hammer, everything looks like a nail."[22] If the only emotion you show is anger, you're going to try and beat people down with it. But no guy would ever try to solve all problems with just a hammer! **You need a whole arsenal of tools available in your garage**. And yes, some are used more than others, but there's always that occasional time when you need that one weird tool and you're glad you kept it all these years! **You need to add tools to your toolbox and then take care of your tools properly. That is the essence of controlling and expressing your emotions.**

As a random side note, guys, the same way you feel about your tools in the garage/shed/workshop, your wife feels about her cooking tools in the kitchen. So, if you ever give her flak for wanting to get a new kitchen gadget, just think how you would feel if she gave you flak for that new garage tool you've been eyeballing. It's a two-way street there, so be kind and respectful to each other about stuff like that. ☺

It's also important to know that depression is very real and as of data from 2017 "322 million people worldwide live with depression."[23] Depression is a chemical imbalance in the brain and is nothing to be ashamed of. Sometimes it can be managed and sometimes it has to be medicated, but either way, it should not be scary or taboo to discuss. When women get depressed, it can often manifest as crying and sadness (along with many other possible responses). Most guys aren't like that, because it seems weak and emotional. The problem is that when guys get depressed, it often manifests with anger, rage, yelling, aggression and violence (along with many other possible responses); but THAT is what is really weak and emotional!! It requires real emotional strength and self-control to combat depression and respond appropriately. But a real man can do it! If you think you may suffer from depression, please talk to someone about it and get help. It's very real and the only weak thing about it is NOT dealing with it properly.

Masculinity is a mask that guys hide behind to avoid going deeper in their relationships or expressing their feelings; but a real man is not afraid of his insides and how they impact his manhood. We have just explored some of the ways that emotional strength is **vital** to manhood. There are others that you can dig into later like: joy, peace, patience, kindness, goodness, faithfulness and gentleness. Go ahead and flex those impressive emotional biceps of yours; <u>doing so will give you the fifth piece of the foundation of manhood.</u>

Chapter Seven:
The Foundation

You may have noticed that I use the word 'intentionally' a lot and that was... intentional. There is nothing about manhood that comes automatically or easy. Manhood doesn't happen by accident. It must be sought after intentionally and you have to desire it. You have to crave it so badly that you are willing to give up the childish ways of boyhood and make the transition. It's time to cross the line and join the tribal hunting party, figuratively.

We now have all of the pieces of the foundation of manhood and are ready to start putting them together to see what it really means to be a MAN: Humility, Wisdom, Discernment, Maturity and Emotional strength. Since we're all guys here and dudes love action and fighting, let's break this down like a boxing match and then see how it applies to our daily life.

Humility: "To know your place." This is the footwork that helps you nimbly maneuver around in the boxing ring. You can dodge out of a situation you shouldn't be in and avoid disaster.

Wisdom: "The ability to apply knowledge to a situation." This is knowing what to hit on your opponent—are you in position for a face punch or just a body jab? This is skill (practical wisdom) and muscle memory (true wisdom) rolled into one package.

Discernment: "The who, where, when and how of what to do." You have to time your punches and blocks properly, or you'll get counterpunched. Wisdom is your greatest offense in this scenario, but discernment allows you to wield it well!

Maturity: "All actions have consequences and mature men take responsibility for their actions." Taking responsibility and acting your age are vital. You wouldn't want to fight a first grader—it's a lose-lose situation. Either you lose to a first grader—wow, just wow—or you beat up a first grader—way to go, jerk face! You should be acting (fighting) your own age (weight class).

Emotional strength: "Self-control flexes your emotional muscles." Maturity has you fighting in the right ring. Humility has you moving in and out of the right situations within the ring. Wisdom is your skill and discernment is your ability to use it. But all of that falls short if you haven't been exercising and strengthening your emotional muscles. This is what gives you the power to control your punches—to hit well or to strategically not hit! Being self-controlled is so important because it helps you control the rest of the pieces by having the strength to make the right decisions that the other pieces show you.

Now let's apply the same principles to something else like interacting with friends or colleagues at work:

Humility: With humility, you're not jealous of those above you or arrogant to those below you. This means you can calmly talk to your superiors and maybe you'll make a positive impression! Or it means you can genuinely talk to your subordinates without being condescending and you may make a great friend or someone that you can mentor!

Wisdom and **Discernment**: If you're in a meeting, it is important to know *what* to say; but it's not just about having the right answer—you have to know *when* to say it and *how* to say it. Saying the right thing at the wrong time can be just as bad as saying the wrong thing at the right time. Your joke may be funny but is it appropriate right then and there?

Maturity: Since 2015, the word "adulting" has exploded in growth of over 600% in social media use.[24] Millennials are entering adult age without any idea of how to do adult things. If you were hiring for a position, would you rather hire a 30-year-old who acts 30, or a 30-year-old who acts 20? How about a 40-year-old who thinks he's still a frat boy in college? I don't know what your job is, but step back and think about your role: if you were your boss, would you hire yourself for your role?

Emotional strength: If a coworker says or does something that angers or offends you, would you rather: A) explode in anger at them and start a fight that accomplishes nothing; or B) calmly pause and explain to them why what they said or did hurt you so that they are aware and won't do it again in the future? Which one has a better outcome? Let's do another one. If someone hurts you, would you rather: A) sit in your office silently stewing on it and ruin your whole day (while they happily move on with life and don't even realize you're emotionally stewing); or B) sit in your office silently choosing to forgive them and releasing the anger and hurt so you can happily move on with life like they are? You don't have to verbally or physically explode with yelling or violence to still let your anger run uncontrolled through your life. Happiness is an emotion that you may or may not be feeling at the time, but **joy is a choice**. We have to intentionally choose joy over the negative alternatives even if it's not what comes naturally or easily. When you choose to be joyful, you chose to refuse to let anger control you. That is being self-controlled; so, flex your emotional biceps and be in charge of your emotional wellbeing.

You must also understand that love is a choice and forgiveness is a choice. There are plenty more like it, but things like these are options that we have to CHOOSE to use or not use. **You *feel* happiness and sadness, but you *choose* joy and love**. If love is just a fleeting feeling then the wind can blow you around and you can "fall out of love" with your wife; but if love is a choice, then you wake up each day and CHOOSE to love your wife and honor the commitment you made to her when you got married. Choose love. Choose joy. Choose forgiveness. If you MAKE yourself choose emotions like these consistently, then they eventually become natural and easy—they become a part of who you are as a man. These are some of the benefits of emotional strength.

I hope you are beginning to understand how humility, wisdom, discernment, maturity and emotional strength all work together to build a solid foundation. Now let's see how that helps us develop true manhood.

True manhood, to put it obviously, is what separates men from boys. True manhood is the difference between being a man and just being a male. As I said at the beginning, being a male is easy. Being a boy is easy. Boys and males do whatever they want; they do whatever feels good at the moment. They don't think about how their decisions, actions, thoughts or words affect other people or even their own future. Life is all about the here and now for them. Men, on the other hand, use their foundation of manhood to analyze a situation and determine the best possible outcome for themselves and those impacted by their decisions and actions. They step up and take ownership and responsibility of themselves and also of those around them. They are strong and courageous but not in an arrogant and cocky way; instead in a humble way because they know their place and are willing to make decisions that may not feel good now, but they know will have a positive impact in the long run.

A real man loves and cares for his family and he's not afraid to show it. He may not cry all of the time, but he's not afraid to show his emotions when the time is right. He has a foundation of manhood that is strong enough to help him lead his family through the good times and the hard times. Life has ups and downs, but a real man stays steadfast through the rough patches like an ocean buoy. The waves may crash up and down, but the buoy holds strong because it is anchored to its foundation. As a man, it is your job to be steadfast for your family—especially when times are tough. That requires really strong emotional muscles and a maturity that sets you apart from childish reactions. Let your wife know that you love her and are there to help and support her. Let your kids know that you love them and are there to protect and guide them. You are the man of the house—it's time to act like a real man!

And a real man doesn't just care for his family in the moment, but instead is constantly looking to the future and is thinking about the legacy that he leaves behind. Is your legacy strong or is it wishy-washy? Do your kids know that you love them and want the best for them? Are your kids in a position to succeed in life thanks to the foundation you have given them? Your legacy is the most important thing you leave behind when you die.

What will others say about you? What will they remember about you? Will they remember you for your yelling and beatings? Or will they remember you for your tenderhearted father's love and protection? Will you leave a wake of destruction that others have to clean up when you're gone? Or will you leave a wake of humility and gratitude for others to enjoy? He who dies with the most toys is, nonetheless, still dead. Make your life matter by leaving a legacy of love and true manhood that you can be proud of.

Any male fool can produce a kid, but a real man takes responsibility for the wellbeing and upbringing of his children. If you have a daughter, you need to treat her as your princess. You should hold her hand tenderly and she should know that her father loves her more than anyone else in the world and if not, she'll seek that fatherly love from other boys—you know what that's like. You should sing to her regularly! She couldn't care less if you sound horrible and are embarrassed; find a song that speaks to her and sing it often—or better yet, write your own song for her and melt her heart with it. It doesn't have to be long or extravagant; the song I made up for my daughter is only four lines long and I just repeat it over and over each day and it's her favorite part of getting ready for bed. If you have a son, you need to treat him as a little man. If you treat him like a boy, he'll stay a boy. It is your job as his father to help him figure out this scary manhood stuff. YOU are the one now that gets to guide him over the line in the sand and build his own foundation of manhood. They're never too young to start learning humility, wisdom, discernment, maturity and emotional strength. Just because you may not have had someone there to guide you through the muddied waters of adolescence doesn't mean he has to suffer the same fate. If you are just now developing this foundation as an adult, just imagine how amazing your son will be with this foundation from his childhood! And this applies to your daughters as well; help them traverse through adolescence and into womanhood as well—even though you are scared out of your mind by it, remember that she is more afraid of it than you are. Be the big man and help guide your children when they need you the most.

So now you've seen the different parts of the foundation of manhood and how all of the parts are integrated and work together. You've seen what it takes and what it means to be a real man. If you step back and look at your life right now, are you humble or do you let jealousy and arrogance make your decisions for you? Are you wise or do you let your foolish nature take over? Do you have understanding and discernment or do you make rash decisions without thinking them through all the way? Do you act your age and own up to your actions or do you display your immaturity for all to see when you blame others and constantly pass the buck of responsibility? Lastly, are you in control of your emotions and not afraid to show them or do you let your emotions control you like a little boy?

I strongly and sincerely challenge you to stop and take an honest look at yourself. This is very serious. Regardless of your age, are you truly a real man or are you just a male pretending to be a man? If not, then don't fear—there is hope! It's never too late to build a foundation of manhood and be a better man!

It's important to note that because these five qualities are so interlocked together to build this foundation that they are best worked on simultaneously; but that doesn't mean you can't focus on one aspect first and improve from there. Just don't get so caught up on one that you ignore the rest; because frankly, you'll never fully be humble, and you'll never be wise enough.

Nobody has ever said "I have officially obtained humility and am now the most humble person in the world!" Right... As a kid, I used to mockingly tell people "I'm more humble than you are!" I was obviously joking and being sarcastic, but it conveyed the point of never really being able to obtain humility without contradicting yourself. We have to constantly strive to be more humble until the day we die—it is a lifelong journey. My new favorite quote is "**obtaining humility is like grabbing a fistful of water; sure, you can do it, but did you really?**" That quote dates all the way back to right now when I just made it up—but it sounds better in quotes, so I'm quoting myself. I'm just that humble! 😉

Also, wisdom and discernment go hand in hand, but Gandhi reminds us that "it is unwise to be too sure of one's own wisdom. It is healthy to be reminded that the strongest might weaken and the wisest might err."[25] And like what Socrates said in the Wisdom chapter, Albert Einstein said, "A true genius admits that he/she knows nothing."[26] So just like with humility, nobody can ever really boast that they are the wisest person ever and no longer need to keep growing! Even King Solomon, who history records as being the wisest person to ever live, spent his whole life seeking more and more wisdom and understanding.

Maturity and Emotional strength are probably the two that are most likely to be "fully obtainable." Maturity is pretty straight forward—are you mature for your age or do you immaturely act in a lower caliber than you should? Likewise, you can be emotionally strong when you've conquered both categories of controlling and expressing your emotions. When you are controlled, you don't overreact, you don't explode, you don't implode—you're levelheaded in your responses. An emotionally controlled person is often a rock for others to hold on to in times of need. They're also a protector or shield for others in times of need. When you're controlled, you're also able to express emotions like kindness and compassion to those who might be hurting around you. Be the one that people can go to for comfort and security!

One of the ways to demonstrate all of the pieces working together is by knowing right from wrong and being able to choose the right thing even in hard times. Some people believe that we are all born naturally good and have good at the center of our hearts—but that is just not true. We are all born with a selfish nature at our core. Just look at toddlers and watch their behaviors; nobody had to teach them to be selfish, rebellious or disobedient. A toddler demonstrates how we all naturally feel: they lie, hit and steal; and they can hurt others without remorse.

All humans naturally feel this way, but children don't have the humility, wisdom, discernment, maturity or emotional strength required to combat the bad nature within us. **By default, we are ALL selfishly "me-minded" but a real man is able to set aside his selfish desires and be selflessly "we-minded" for the benefit of others first**. Don't just say "at least I'm not as bad as Hitler!" and think that makes you good—there are no perfect people and we are all bad (some more than others) and need to make a conscience choice to do the right things each day.

THAT is the foundation of manhood that we should all strive for. *Remember, a real man is always a male, but a male is not always a real man.* **Manhood doesn't happen by accident. True manhood takes *intentional determination* and *ongoing hard work*.** You must work on building it daily—for the rest of your life! And fortunately, you now have the right tools that you need to do so! Nothing is stopping you from being the MAN that you can be.

Chapter Eight:
Building Time!

Manhood can take a lot of different shapes and forms throughout different cultures, so I'm not trying to pigeonhole it into a specific box or label; but instead I'm trying to break apart the false presumptions that come with manhood just being tied to masculinity. My main goal is to build this universal foundation that all guys should strive for and grow in.

Now that we have a foundation of manhood to stand on, let's start building on that. There are other aspects to manhood that I didn't dig into because I feel that those are best acquired and cultivated once you have a strong foundation of the others. This is a paraphrase from author Glenn Stanton: “While certainly not exhaustive or comprehensive, this list is a compilation of many of the most important, widely practiced and culturally expected qualities of manhood according to cultural anthropologists, psychologists and sociologists who have studied the nature of manhood across diverse cultures and time:

Communicative: A man is able to communicate efficiently and effectively. He is open and sincere about his thoughts and feelings without shoving down his emotions internally and hiding them. He can openly express ideas without rejecting criticism or feedback.

Compassion: This might seem feminine, but a man sees the struggles of the weak and those in trouble and readily comes to their aid. This is a moral strength. A man doesn't exploit an innocent person's weakness.

Courage: A man does not shrink from a necessary challenge, regardless of risk. He will face danger, difficulty and self-denial when called upon for the sake of others.

Integrity: A man does what is right and calls out others who do not. He deals with others honestly and doesn’t lie—either through *commission* (saying something untrue) or *omission* (*not* saying something that *is* true). Temptation presents itself to every man, but the decisions and actions he takes in light of it significantly determines his manhood. He can be trusted to do what is right when no one is watching. He keeps his word and is dependable to others.

Listener: A man can listen to others. Greek philosopher, Epictetus, said, 'We have two ears and one mouth so that we can listen twice as much as we speak.'[27] During a conversation, a man honestly listens to the other person and doesn't just focus on his rebuttal or next point.

Loyalty: A man is loyal to his family, friends and others who are close to him, even at a great price to himself.

Meekness: A man is meek and gentle. Meek is commonly called weak; but it is not at all. Meek means having strength under control. Just because you have the power or ability to do something, doesn't mean you have to do it. A man is controlled and gentle, especially with those who are not as strong as him.

Observant: A man pays attention to what is going on around him and doesn't get blindsided. When he sees an issue or need, he fixes it. When he's driving, he's not going 15mph *under* the speed limit in the *left* lane (you know who you are...).

Respect: A man shows respect to himself and those he meets, regardless of their station. He looks them in the eye. He gives another man a firm handshake. He offers words of respect such as 'Yes, sir/ma'am' or 'Thank you, sir/ma'am.' A man helps others feel valuable. **He is a real gentleman in the truest sense of the word**.

Secure: A man is secure in himself and does not let his own insecurities or other people dictate his own thoughts, words and actions. A man stands firm in what he knows and believes.

Self-Reliance: A man can stand on his own and not need to depend on others for his well-being. The Boy Scout motto is 'Be Prepared' because a man doesn't want to have to depend on the preparedness of another. He is not a loner though. He is willing to work with others.

Step Up: A man is the first one out of his seat (figuratively and literally) when a need arises. He's a problem solver and takes initiative. Passivity is never manly.

Tenacity: A man does not easily give up or shrink away in the face of challenge or adversity. He sticks with it and wants to overcome obstacles. 'It can't be done' doesn't come to him easily."[28] A man is a hard worker through and through.

Thermostat: A thermometer checks the temperature; a thermostat **sets** the temperature. A man does not passively reflect his surroundings, but instead he actively sets the tone for those around him. This doesn't mean that he is always domineering or loud, but it means he can influence others with a strong will and a level head when necessary.

Trainable: A man is humble enough to know that he doesn't know everything and is not always right and therefore he is teachable or trainable. He listens to the advice of others and is willing to learn from them. The hardest part of this is when you must learn from someone younger than yourself—but a man can do it!

Vision: A man has vision for his future and knows where he wants to end up. He doesn't let the wind blow him wherever it wants. When the waves of life crash against him, he has a strong rudder to keep himself on course towards his destination in life. A man without vision is a man without a mission.

Vocal Filter: A man chooses his words carefully when he speaks. He has a filter in place between his brain and his mouth and doesn't just spit out everything that comes through his head. Words have power and he wields that power wisely and doesn't let his loose lips sink ships.

As you can see, there are many different aspects of manhood that set it apart from just simply being a male. Again, being a male is easy; being a man is hard and requires intentional effort—but it is so worth it!

One timely example of combining these traits is a man who is capable of having a strong-willed but completely civil discussion or disagreement about politics or religion without resulting in arguing, yelling, name calling or getting derogatory in any way. It has become common place that if someone doesn't agree with you, they are instantly a horrible person and you would be a horrible person for *not* yelling at them and making sure they know they're a horrible person. But that is so unmanly that it is not even funny. You don't need to get offended or angry just because someone disagrees with you on something. **Getting easily offended at everything shows a *lack* of emotion strength**. Debating with other people is great but stay controlled, level-headed and respectful and be a real man!

Once you have a solid foundation to start with, you can the proceed to build up your manhood like a castle. You wouldn't build a castle on the sand of a beach, would you? That would be horrible and never last. A building as majestic as a castle needs a STRONG foundation for it to stand the test of time and turbulence. I grew up playing with LEGOs® and got really good at building strong structures once I learned how to build on a base and work up. Start with the five pieces of the foundation of manhood and then build on that everything that you want to express to others! Be strong and courageous! Be caring and kind! Be honest and driven! Be a real MAN!

If you're a single guy, then work on improving yourself *before* pursuing a woman. Do you want a wife that just settles for an average male or do you want a wife that insists on being loved and appreciated by a real man? Now is the time to work on improving yourself and create an awesome future built on your foundation of manhood!

If you're married, then be the man that your family wants and needs you to be! **Marriage is never easy because nobody is perfect, but that's why we *make a vow up front* to commit to working on relationship**! *Choose* to love your wife each day and stay devoted to her and your family. Family is everything. <u>If you have sons</u>, then help guide them into their own manhood from an early age. <u>If you have daughters</u>, then help them see what a real man should be before they settle for just an average male of their own. You desperately need to understand the vital role that you play in your children's lives. Fatherlessness and the broken home that it causes has reached a critical point in history. Suzanne Venker, an author of five books on feminism and gender politics, wrote in a blog post:

"[Fatherlessness] is destructive to both boys and girls, but each sex suffers differently. Girls who grow up deprived of their father are more likely to become depressed, more likely to self-harm, and more likely to be promiscuous. But they still have their mothers, with whom they clearly identify. Boys do not have a comparable identification and thus suffer more from father absence. They also tend to act out in a manner that's harmful to others, which girls typically do not.

The root of fatherlessness rests in two things: our culture's dismissal of men as valuable human beings who have something unique to offer, and its dismissal of marriage as an institution that's crucial to the health and well-being of children."[29]

Fatherhood is so critical, but you need a solid foundation of manhood to build fatherhood on. Your children will be looking up to you for an example of how to live their lives. **Your sons will want to be just like you**, so make sure that you're setting an example that you want them to follow! **Your daughters will be naturally inclined to find a husband with**

your values and foundation, so make sure your you're demonstrating what you want them to look for in a real man. As a father, YOU are the MAN of the house! Are you willing to step up to the plate and lead them?

Another aspect of fatherhood is in being a father-figure to other's kids as well. That means if there's a boy on your street that doesn't have a dad, you step in and be an example for him. It doesn't mean you have to replace his dad, but maybe (with his mom's permission), you just take him out for a slice of pizza once a month or something. Everyone needs an older guy to talk to, so you be there for him if he needs to talk. You can treat someone like your own son even if they're not and both of your lives will be better for it in the end. It takes a village to raise a kid sometimes. Be that village and make a difference.

This book is short because manhood isn't complicated when it's broken down into simple parts and analyzed. Now that you've read it and grasped a better understanding of yourself and your manhood; I dare you to go back and read it again. Knowing the ending will let you dig deeper into the parts that you may have glazed over the first time. It's like watching a movie again to catch all of the Easter eggs that you missed the first time! You can do it! Enjoy!

[**SIDE NOTE TO WOMEN**: I am in no way trying to belittle single moms or women that are trying to make it on their own. Single moms are real life superheroes in my book, and I know I couldn't do what you do—so thank you for your sacrifices. Fatherlessness doesn't just impact the kids, but it impacts you as well, and for that I am truly sorry. Whether you feel that you can do it all on your own or you feel that you can't do it at all, there will be times that you may need to get help from a trustworthy real man in the village to step in and help—please don't turn away good help, but also please don't just let any male strut in and take your kids under his wing without making sure he has his own solid foundation of manhood. The man you let mentor your kids will directly impact your kid's foundations and the rest of their lives.

Additionally, you may have noticed that a lot of what we have discussed as the foundation of manhood also applies to your foundation of womanhood and that's true. Please don't feel like this is strictly limited to guys alone; but women are naturally better at things like expressing emotions, humility and maturity. Guys need a lot more help building their foundations; hence this book is primarily directed at helping guys. I hope you are able to take what you've learned here and apply it to your life as well! You are just as important and necessary!]

Chapter Nine:
The End

Congratulations! You have made it to the bonus round! If you've made it this far, it must mean that you're really hungry for true manhood and are willing to dive in deeper to figure it out and grow stronger! The best way to succeed at this new adventure is to not do it alone. Find another guy near you that wants to build the foundation of his manhood as well and the two of you can help build each other up. One of King Solomon's most commonly quoted lines is "As iron sharpens iron, so one man sharpens another."[30] So find someone around you that can sharpen you while you sharpen him. Or better yet, find a bunch of guys and create your own Brotherhood of Real Men that can help each other! Nobody, no matter how strong or tough or well founded, can succeed in becoming a real man on their own.

You might think this is too hard to do on your own or you just don't know where to start. "Philip, you just don't understand what I've been through or what I've done..." And you're right—I might not. That's why there's an incredible organization that meets locally in 35,000 locations called Celebrate Recovery (CR). CR is a safe and welcoming place for anyone who is struggling to be free from a hurt, habit or hang-up. (Which is all of us!) Take a bold step towards being a man and attend a meeting. You can go to www.CelebrateRecovery.com for a location near you.

For more amazing insight into true manhood and fatherhood, **I HIGHLY recommend a movie called COURAGEOUS**. I have no affiliation with the movie, but it has touched me and inspired me to be a better man and father and I want everyone to get to experience it as well.

Now allow me the last few pages to take this in a different direction. As I mentioned in the wisdom chapter, true wisdom comes from seeking God and asking Him for it. If you don't believe that or if you don't even believe that God exists, there is so much awesomeness that you're missing out on! You can never reach the full greatness of real manhood without the grace of God and the endless love that He pours out on you. Once you experience the incredible love of God, it will make it so much easier and natural for you to pour out the same love on your family.

If this overflowing love of God intrigues you or you're just curious about who God is or if he even exists, you can call or text and talk to someone right now at (320) 345-3455. Or go to www. ChatAboutFaith.com. You can also go to www.CRU.org and click on *How to Know God Personally*. It will change your life in ways you can't even imagine! There is nothing you need to do to earn God's love and forgiveness besides trust in Him!!

I pray that you honestly desire to do everything you can to become the real man that your family wants and needs you to be. Ask God to help you build your foundation of manhood and strive to be the MAN that we both know you can be! Thanks for going on this journey with me.

-Philip

"Remember, dear brothers, that few of you were wise in the world's eyes or powerful or wealthy when God called you. Instead, God chose things the world considers foolish in order to shame those who think they are wise. And he chose things that are powerless to shame those who are powerful. God chose things despised by the world, things counted as nothing at all, and used them to bring to nothing what the world considers important. As a result, no one can ever boast in the presence of God." [31]

The Life and Legacy of My Prince

A Letter From Philip's Wife

6/18/1987–9/5/2019

Philip Ganzfried was and will always be the LOVE of my life. He was my true prince, a protector, a provider, a comforter, a source of laughter, and my best friend.

I am sitting here in his favorite spot, one month after he tragically passed away in his sleep without warning. My heart is heavy with grief, but I want to share with you the man he was and the impact he will have for eternity. He finished this book just weeks before he passed away, and he was so excited to hold his author copies. He had talked about writing these things down for our entire eight years of marriage. He joked about how ironic it was that God was using him to write a book.

You see, he hated to read books, and he was open about that. He loved learning and growing, but he would do that through reading articles, videos, and listening to audio lessons while he was driving. He knew God was up to something big when he was inspired to write a book! You see, he didn't just write words on mere paper—he lived and breathed what he wrote about in this book. Everything in this book was from his heart, and he wrote it because God told him to share it with others. He truly was a man after God's own heart, and I got to witness it at the deepest level over the last nine years.

My prince walked the walk and lived a transparent life of integrity. Now, don't get me wrong, he would be the first person to tell you that in no way was he perfect. He knew that he was a flawed, sinful man who was saved by God's grace. He was chosen and forgiven by his Lord, and he strived daily to live his life honoring his Heavenly Father.

Did he make mistakes? Yes, but he humbled himself and would own up to them. He took responsibility for his actions. He always shared openly about his struggle with pride. He was a brilliant man and even made it into Mensa. He would jokingly say, "I am more humble than you are!" He knew that his mind and abilities were God given, and he wanted to keep his mind and pride in check on a daily basis.

He could do the Rubik's cube in less than two minutes, despite the fact that he was color blind, and just for kicks, he would finish it behind his back to show off! A few of his flaws included a hate for exercise (ironically, he married a personal trainer and athlete), never eating his vegetables (he would physically gag), loving sweets a little too much, and being tone deaf. But even that didn't stop him from singing out loud to his Lord! Philip also really had no fashion sense.

I am telling you about these flaws not to tear him down but to tell you that he didn't focus on the negative effects of these flaws—instead he strived to improve on his weaknesses. I was always amazed how in our marriage he was the first to ask for forgiveness. He wouldn't allow his emotions to overtake him, even if he was hurt or in pain.

In eight years of marriage and almost nine years of knowing him, we never went to bed angry. He made sure that no matter what, we always talked things out, prayed together, and that anger and resentment was never left to fester. The glue that bonded us from the first day that we started dating was the fact that we made it an absolute priority to pray together every single night, and we only missed a handful of nights in nine years. You truly get to know someone when you hear them pouring out their praises, fears, concerns, and desires to their God.

My love was a strong-willed go-getter who went after what he wanted, especially if it was something he knew God was laying on his heart. Our love story is a testament to that. I will share more details in the future on our website, but Philip and I both held strongly to our God-given convictions throughout our teen and college years, and we both waited for each other. I never wanted to settle for any guy. I wanted a man of God, someone who put God first in his life. We both looked for someone who was spiritually wise and who had the qualities that we wanted in our future spouse. We prayed and waited for each other for twenty-five years.

Once he came into my life, we both knew that our years of praying, sacrificing, and waiting had finally paid off. God knew exactly the man that I needed; he created Philip for me. We had a lot of smaller differences, but we were on the same page on the big things in life. After waiting so long to find each other, we decided to save our first kiss for the wedding altar. You grow emotionally and spiritually very close to someone when you are dating them and you save sex for the marriage bed. Our marriage wasn't perfect, it was not a fairytale, but it was a God-honoring marriage where two flawed people came together to pursue God and to walk through life's ups and downs together with an unwavering commitment to each other.

My protector was always a big, strong guy. And yet, he was tender and caring, and he gave the best hugs. He had a smile and eyes that would light up a room. He was the best father to our two young kids, who are two and four years old. He could swaddle a baby like a champ. He was so good with babies; I was so impressed. Whenever I was sleep-deprived and moody the past five years, he showed me so much grace and always helped me whenever he was able. He sacrificed so much of his own sleep and time for our family.

As the kids got older in the past few years, he would spend hours playing with them, building things and exploring. As a kid he loved LEGOs, robots, video games, and anything techy, and he was excited to pass those passions on to our kids! We would welcome him home from work, and he would get on their level and love on them, then play. He would read them Bible stories before bed. He would sing goodnight songs and pray over them every night. He showered them with love and grace. He was the most patient daddy, and he inspired me with how he could remain calm during life's crazy chaotic days and weeks.

He was always teaching them how to use gadgets and how to make and improve things, He wanted them to know how much he loved and cherished them. He truly adored his role as father, and he wanted them to know that his family was his top priority. He took this role very seriously. He was our provider and protector, and he would do whatever it took to honor his commitments and carry out his God-given role.

Our provider loved to invent and make things more efficient. His end goal of all his jobs was to streamline and make things more efficient. He had hundreds of inventive ideas throughout our marriage, the majority stayed in his mind, but he had a few that he was seriously passionate about, and he was diligently working on to make them happen.

He bought a 3D printer a few months ago and was creating prototypes for one invention. I will try to make those ideas happen in the future. He was wise financially, content in life, and didn't need much to be happy. Giving was a top priority in his life. He always made sure we gave tithes and offerings first. He had what he called a "God fund," where we put money away to randomly bless people with when God showed us who and when.

It was so exciting to be married to such a wise giver! He flipped his first house right after we got married, and we have bought and sold three other homes in eight years. We followed the Dave Ramsey financial plan to work hard and get out of debt so that we could live and give like no one else. He loved working, and he always brought humor and fun to his jobs. He worked incredibly hard, but he also knew how to throw in a joke at the perfect time to make anyone from the janitor to the CEO laugh. At his last three jobs, he even convinced the top dogs to allow his office to have Nerf gun wars! He loved running around the office shooting his co-workers, having random battles with his co-workers to lighten the stress load.

Philip worked smart and was succeeding in all that he set out to accomplish. This past June, he hit five years at his current job, and he felt a strong peace that his time there was coming to an end. It was an undeniable peace that he kept talking about all summer. He was so excited about what God had in store for him.

On September 3rd, 2019, he interviewed for an amazing job at Dave Ramsey's headquarters. We felt God's presence, and we thought we would be moving to Tennessee this fall. Two days later, when we returned home, he passed away in his sleep. His time working on earth had come to an end abruptly, but his greatest life was just starting.

Philip's thirty-two years of life had one theme and mission. He knew from an early age that he was a child of God, saved by Grace, and that his purpose and mission on earth was to bring glory and honor to his Heavenly Father with his talents and abilities. He was wise beyond his years. His favorite place and where he felt the most alive was when he was worshiping his God up near the front row in church. He didn't care what anyone thought—his heart was praising his creator. He would raise his hands, go on his knees, and just worship his God. He was in awe of God's greatness.

He was always so thankful for the amazing earthly parents that God had given him. He lived to honor, respect, and love them. Tom (Dad) and Maria (Mom) poured out their lives to teach and demonstrate

God's love and grace to their four kids. He made his love and respect known to them whenever he had a chance. His father was one of his best friends, and his mother had his heart for life! Philip was an amazing big brother to his three younger sisters. He truly loved them, protected them, and enjoyed all his years being their big brother. He was so proud to watch them grow into amazing women of God who were serving and fulfilling their unique purposes in life.

He was a true friend to those who were able to know him. He would give his time to help anyone who asked for tech help, or he would stop and pray for anyone if they needed it. Philip fit perfectly in with my family from the moment they met him. It was a seamless transition having him in our lives. He was one of a kind. Philip knew that you can never outgive God in life and that if God laid it on your heart to give something away, it would rock your world to obey! In high school, he created this mission statement, and he kept it on a card in his wallet.

Philip Ganzfried's MISSION STATEMENT:

"I will be a man of God whose heart is always bigger than my wallet—no matter how big my wallet gets—because my purpose in life is to advance the Kingdom of God by financially supporting the men and women that passionately pursue Jesus Christ and take his life-giving message to the ends of the earth!"

Philip didn't know that his earthly life would end so quickly. None of us expected this, and it is so shocking and painful to lose such an amazing man so abruptly. But know this: We have hope in the God who created Philip, the God who knows all, and who is using Philip's life even now to carry out His divine purpose. Philip is now in his happy place, worshiping his Lord, hands held high for eternity. He would want you to really look at your life and ask God to show Himself to you.

You were created for a purpose. You are unique, and you have a lot to offer the world, but you have to choose daily to take the steps to become the man or woman that God created you to be. Will it be challenging? Absolutely. But it will be worth the effort! I ask that in honor of Philip, you take a leap of faith and ask God to show Himself to you today. Philip prayed for you as he was writing this book, and it is by no coincidence that you are reading this. You are the one that he prayed God would use his words to impact.

We look forward to hearing about your journey and will continue to share Philip's life and legacy.

Sincerely,
Jennifer Ganzfried

Check out more about Philip's life and his mission in the coming months at:

www.ManOrMaleTheBook.com

https://www.facebook.com/Man-or-Male-108675870535573/

A Letter from Pastor Rick Keaton

October 2019

Philip,

When Jennifer brought you into our family's life, it was a seamless transition. Because of the way you were raised, family was always important to you. You welcomed us as your second family, just as we welcomed you, and it felt like you had always been one of us.

When you emailed me the rough draft of your book this summer, I was able to read it on a flight home. I was really impressed with the simple, straightforward wisdom coming from someone your age. Wisdom is usually garnered as we grow older, but you were half my age.

Just two weeks before your untimely passing, you sat in our living room with an author's pre-published hard copy, and you were beaming from ear to ear. Rightly so, because it was a tremendous accomplishment. I only wish I had known that it would be one of the last times I would see you face-to-face. I would have given you a great big bear hug and told you how proud we all were of this accomplishment. No one knew we wouldn't have another chance.

As I prepared to speak at your memorial service, I reread your book and came to the realization that even at the young age of thirty-two, you lived and embodied every one of the principles you wrote about. Your challenge to every male can be achieved!

Philip, I am very proud of you, and you were the MAN that you wrote about. Until we meet again.

Love you and miss you already!
Pastor Rick Keaton
Father-in-Law

A Letter from Noah Lowder

Thank you for reading these final words from Philip. These words were not mere words to him—this was how Philip lived his life. Philip leaves behind a legacy of caring for his family in each moment as well as preparing them for the future. He will be remembered for his tenderhearted father's love and protection. He leaves a legacy of a wonderful family who loves Jesus and loves others well. A legacy of confident humility and gratitude. He leaves a legacy of being a brother and friend to many.

Philip has been my friend and brother for over a decade. I had the honor of being his best man at his wedding, and he was the best man in mine.

If I could only use one word to describe Philip, it would be faithful. He was a faithful Christ follower, faithful husband, faithful father, faithful brother, faithful friend. He taught me what genuine brotherly love was. He cheered me at my best and stood with me at my worst. God used his friendship to teach me what it meant to be there for someone. To love people where they are, to be unmoved and unfazed by their shortcomings or sin, and also how to encourage and challenge them without shame. Philip was steadfast and loyal. He was the type of friend I now always strive to be.

He was a faithful man because of his faith in his Lord and Savior Jesus Christ. His hope is in Jesus.

He believed in what he wrote in this book. It was because of this hope and faith that he was the man he was and left the legacy he did. I encourage every man (and woman) reading this book to earnestly take the principles in this book to heart, to consider the legacy they will leave, and to know that the hope Philip had in Christ Jesus is open to all who seek Him.

Noah Lowder

Resources

For more information, check out these resources below. I have no affiliation with any of them but found them all useful on my journey. I hope you will as well.

Books, movies and articles:

- A movie about true manhood and fatherhood: www.AffirmFilms.com/movie/COURAGEOUS
- A book with a more in-depth dive into humility: Humility: True Greatness by C. J. Mahaney
- A book on controlling your emotions: Happiness Is a Choice by Minirth and Meier
- Article on the effects of fatherlessness: www.FoxNews.com/opinion/missing-fathers-and-americas-broken-boys-the-vast-majority-of-mass-shooters-come-from-broken-homes
- Videos digging into common questions about life: www.TheTruthProject.org

People to contact for help:

- Get help or find a local group of dads in your area:
  - www.CityDadsGroup.com
  - www.AllProDad.com
- A safe place where guys help guys grow as real men:
  - www.CelebrateRecovery.com
- Find out more about God and His love:
  - www.NeedHim.org or (320) 345-3455
  - www.CRU.org
  - www.ChatAboutFaith.com

References

1 Falsely attributed to CS Lewis, this quote was actually from Ken Blanchard in 1990 or Rich Howard and Jamie Lash in 1992. It's also attributed to Rick Warren in 2002.
2 www.brainyquote.com/quotes/ernest_hemingway_174758
3 Mark Twain (2013). "Delphi Complete Works of Mark Twain (Illustrated)", p.8840, Delphi Classics
4 www.brainyquote.com/quotes/socrates_101212
5 Proverbs 11:2 (NLT)
6 Proverbs 2:6 (NIV), Proverbs 16:16 (Paraphrased), Proverbs 19:8 (NIV), Proverbs 12:15 (NIV).
7 www.practicalbusinessideas.com/king-solomon-wealth-net-worth
8 Proverbs 2:2 (ESV), 1:7b (ESV), 2:6 (ESV), 3:13 (ESV), 10:13 (ESV), 18:2a (ESV), Psalm 32:9 (NIV)
9 James 3:13 (NIV)
10 www.twitter.com/ChadSVCC/status/1160342052791414784
11 www.daveramsey.com/company/faq
12 www.brainyquote.com/quotes/oscar_wilde_100487
13 Proverbs 29:11 (ESV)
14 www.brainyquote.com/quotes/theodore_hesburgh_114459
15 1 Samuel 17:34-37 (NLT)
16 1 Samuel 17 (NLT)
17 www.britannica.com/biography/David www.ancient.eu/King_David
18 1 Samuel 21:11 (NLT) and 1 Chronicles 19:17-19 (NLT)
19 Psalm 6:6 (NLT)
20 Psalms 3-9; 11-41; 51-65; 68-70; 86; 101; 103; 108-110; 122; 124; 131; 133; and 138-145.
21 www.smithsonianmag.com/arts-culture/to-be-or-not-to-be-shakespeare-127247606
22 Abraham H. Maslow (1966). The Psychology of Science. p. 15.
23 www.adaa.org/understanding-anxiety/depression
24 www.merriam-webster.com/words-at-play/adulting
25 www.brainyquote.com/quotes/mahatma_gandhi_150732
26 www.azquotes.com/quote/361652

27 www.brainyquote.com/quotes/epictetus_106298
28 www.focusonthefamily.com/about/focus-findings/the-nature-of-manhood/what-are-the-universal-qualities-of-manhood
29 www.foxnews.com/opinion/missing-fathers-and-americas-broken-boys-the-vast-majority-of-mass-shooters-come-from-broken-homes
30 Proverbs 27:17 (NIV)
31 1 Corinthians 1:26-29 (NLT)

If you have any questions at all about these sources, please, please call (320) 345-3455 and you can anonymously ask someone every question you can think of. Someone is waiting to help answer your questions right now! God bless!

Made in the USA
Monee, IL
24 June 2020